Contents

Introduction 2

Main Letter-Sound Spellings 5
s, a, t, i, p, n, c k, e, h 6
r, m, d, g 8
o, u, l 10
f, b, ai, j 12
oa, ie, ee, or 14
z, w, ng, v 16
oo, **oo**, y, x 18
ch, sh, th, **th** 20
qu, ou, oi, ue 22
er, ar 24

Alternative Letter-Sound Spellings 26
‹y› as /ee/ 27
‹a_e› as /ai/, ‹e_e› as /ee/ 28
‹i_e› as /ie/, ‹o_e› as /oa/ 30
‹u_e› as /ue/, ‹ay› as /ai/, ‹oy› as /oi/, ‹ea› as /ee/ ... 32
‹y› as /ie/, ‹igh› as /ie/, ‹ow› as /oa/, ‹ow› as /ou/ 34
‹ir› as /er/, ‹ur› as /er/, ‹ew› as /ue/, ‹aw› as /or/ 36
‹au› as /or/, ‹al› as /or/, ‹ph› as /f/, soft ‹c› 38
soft ‹g›, ‹ue› as /oo/, ‹u_e› as /oo/, ‹ew› as /oo/ 40
‹air› as /air/, ‹ear› as /air/, ‹are› as /air/ 42

Tricky Words 44
Extra Practice 46

Introduction

The Jolly Phonics Word Bank is a useful tool for teachers to use with Jolly Phonics. As teaching progresses and new letter sounds are introduced, new words become available for blending, segmenting and writing. The Word Bank covers spellings for the 42 main letter sounds before moving on to cover alternative letter-sound spellings. Alternative letter-sound spellings are only suitable for blending, segmenting and dictation when they are the focus of the lesson.

Reading and Writing

In Jolly Phonics, children are taught to read by blending letter sounds together to form words, so that /c-a-t/ becomes *cat*. At the same time, they are taught to write by segmenting words into letter sounds, so that *dog* is understood to be made up of the sounds /d-o-g/.

The Purpose of the Jolly Phonics Word Bank

In the early stages of learning to read and write, it is important that children are given sufficient blending, segmenting and writing practice, especially children who are slow to start. In order to achieve this, it is helpful for teachers to have a bank of words which only use letter sounds once they have been taught.

The aim of this Word Bank is to provide a large selection of words to choose from to support teaching and activities in the classroom. Phrases and sentences have been included where appropriate as an example of how the Word Bank can be used to create suitable sentences for blending.

Each entry in the Word Bank is divided into four rows:

1. Words for blending, segmenting and dictation

Words in this section are completely regular and can be reliably blended, segmented and used for dictation. Once a word has been blended a few times it becomes 'known' and then blending is only needed for new words that are not yet known. Once they are confident at blending, encourage the children to blend the sounds silently in their head and just say the word.

2. Words for blending only

Words in this section are suitable for blending but not dictation, for example:
- Words which contain the letter sound /ck/, which may be spelt with a ‹c›, ‹k› or ‹ck›. Initially, children use the ‹c› spelling for the /ck/ sound until they have been taught the rules linked to the ‹k› and ‹ck› spellings.
- Words which contain double consonants (e.g. *bell, miss*). The sounds can be identified in these words but the children do not know, at this stage, that some of the consonants need to be doubled.
- Proper nouns (e.g. *June, Luke*).

3. Challenging words for blending

These words contain something that is not completely regular which needs a small 'tweak' to hear the word. For example:
- Words which contain a schwa or a swallowed vowel sound (e.g. *doct<u>or</u>, lem<u>o</u>n, <u>a</u>bout, harv<u>e</u>st, pock<u>e</u>t*).
- Words which contain the spelling pattern ‹nk› (e.g. *pi<u>n</u>k, tha<u>n</u>k*), as the ‹n› makes an /ng/ sound here.
- Words in which ‹s› is pronounced as /z/ (e.g. *i<u>s</u>, dog<u>s</u>, wi<u>s</u>e*).
- Words which end in ‹l› or ‹r›, producing a schwa sound (e.g. *craw<u>l</u>, poo<u>l</u>, fue<u>l</u>, hea<u>l</u>, clea<u>r</u>, ow<u>l</u>, sou<u>r</u>, cur<u>l</u>*).

The 'challenging' parts of words are underlined in the Word Bank so that teachers can easily identify which parts children may struggle with. For example, the word *revise* is presented as 'r<u>e</u>vi<u>s</u>e'.

4. Phrases and sentences for reading

Each new entry provides some simple phrases and sentences for children to blend and read once the appropriate letter sounds and tricky words have been taught. Teachers can use the Word Bank to make up their own phrases and sentences.

Tricky Words

Tricky words are common words that are needed to make simple sentences. They either have an alternative spelling that has not been taught yet or a phonic irregularity, which makes them more difficult for children to read and spell. Tricky words are introduced into the phrases and sentences section according to where they are taught within Jolly Phonics, and appear in **bold**. After three entries, tricky words are treated as 'known' and are no longer presented in bold. Care should be taken, when dictating sentences, that only tricky words that have been taught are used. There is a complete list of the 72 tricky words taught in Jolly Phonics on pages 44-45.

Main Letter-Sound Spellings

Group 1	s	a	t	i	p	n
Group 2	c k	e	h	r	m	d
Group 3	g	o	u	l	f	b
Group 4	ai	j	oa	ie	ee	or
Group 5	z	w	ng	v	oo	oo
Group 6	y	x	ch	sh	th	th
Group 7	qu	ou	oi	ue	er	ar

s a t i p n c k e h r m d g o u l f b ai j oa

s, a
(No words are available for blending at this stage.)

t
Words for blending, segmenting and dictation
sat at

i
Words for blending, segmenting and dictation
sit it its

Challenging words for blending
assist is

p
Words for blending, segmenting and dictation
pip pit pat tap sap tip sip spit spat

Challenging words for blending
pasta

n
Words for blending, segmenting and dictation
nap nip nit pan pin tan tin tint spin pant snap snip span an in ant insist

Challenging words for blending
assistant

Phrases and sentences for reading
a tin   a pan   tip tap   snip snap   ants in pants   an ant in a tin

ie ee or z w ng v oo **oo** y x ch sh th **th** qu ou oi ue er ar

c k

Words for blending, segmenting and dictation
cat can cap scan act panic picnic tact

Words for blending only
kit skip skin napkin tick pick pack kick sick sack stick snack stack

Challenging words for blending
ki<u>ss</u> a<u>t</u>tic i<u>n</u>k ta<u>n</u>k pi<u>n</u>k sa<u>n</u>k si<u>n</u>k sti<u>n</u>k spa<u>n</u>k a<u>tt</u>a<u>ck</u>

Phrases and sentences for reading
a cat   a picnic   a pi<u>n</u>k cap   a sick cat   Pack a snack.

e

Words for blending, segmenting and dictation
set pet net pen ten test pest nest sent step tent spent insect inspect

Words for blending only
neck peck kept speck tennis

Challenging words for blending
<u>a</u>rrest

Phrases and sentences for reading
a neck   a pet cat   ten steps   a tennis kit   an insect in a tent

h

Words for blending, segmenting and dictation
hen hat hip hit hint hectic

Words for blending only
hiss

Challenging words for blending
ha<u>s</u> happ<u>e</u>n

Phrases and sentences for reading
a hat   ten hats   a hint   a cat in a hat   a hen in a pen

s a t i p n c k e h **r** m d g o u l f b ai j oa

r

Words for blending, segmenting and dictation

rat rip ran rest trap trip rent strip strap print spirit crisp scrap strict crept

Words for blending only

rack risk prick press stress track trick

Challenging words for blending

ri<u>n</u>k pre<u>s</u>ent re<u>s</u>pect re<u>s</u>ist rack<u>e</u>t crick<u>e</u>t <u>a</u>ttract actr<u>e</u>ss transpar<u>e</u>nt

Phrases and sentences for reading

a pet rat   rest in a nest   a rip in a hat   cracks in a pan
A cat crept in an attic.

m

Words for blending, segmenting and dictation

man men map mat hem ram him rim mist mint trim pram stem tram prim imp stamp tramp tempt camp mimic

Words for blending only

miss mess mass smack

Challenging words for blending

mi<u>n</u>k <u>a</u>ttem<u>p</u>t mattr<u>e</u>ss

Phrases and sentences for reading

a man   ten men   a mess   a cat on a mat   A man camps in a tent.

ie ee or z w ng v oo **oo** y x ch sh th **th** qu ou oi ue er ar

d

Words for blending, segmenting and dictation
dad den did dip sad rid red mad had hid din pad dim mid sand
mend send dent tend hand damp drip disc and end spend stand
timid intend rapid dentist drastic handstand

Words for blending only
kid deck skid desk dress disk add addict

Challenging words for blending
dri<u>n</u>k dra<u>n</u>k pand<u>a</u> <u>a</u>ddress pr<u>e</u>tend <u>a</u>ttend <u>a</u>dapt <u>a</u>dmit

Phrases and sentences for reading
a dri<u>n</u>k   a red dress   a handstand
A tap drips.   Mend a hat.   A rat did a trick.

g

Words for blending, segmenting and dictation
gas peg gap get dig rag rig sag tag nag drag snag crag grip grin
stag gram grim grand grandad

Words for blending only
egg

Challenging words for blending
magn<u>e</u>t an<u>a</u>gram

Phrases and sentences for reading
a grin   ten gram<u>s</u>   a tent peg   a gap in a tent   Grandad i<u>s</u> sad.

9

s a t i p n c k e h r m d g o u l f b ai j oa

o

Words for blending, segmenting and dictation
top pop pot pod hot hop rot rod dog dot got cot cod cog not nod mop on pond spot stop trod trot drop crop comic topic

Words for blending only
odd rock sock cross dock mock cannot desktop tick-tock

Challenging words for blending
<u>a</u>dopt <u>a</u>cross ho<u>n</u>k rock<u>et</u> pock<u>et</u> spott<u>ed</u> okr<u>a</u>

Phrases and sentences for reading
a hot pot   top tips   a hotdog   a dog dig<u>s</u>   moss on a rock
a rock in a pond   an odd sock

u

Words for blending, segmenting and dictation
cup cut hum tug mud sun run rut pup sum nut nun gum mug dug pun hunt dump dust must gust rust drum snug drug spun rump pump hump stump crust scrub trust grunt upset mumps undid sunset suntan instruct product

Words for blending only
putt muck suck tuck duck dusk tusk stuck pumpkin hiccup eggcup discuss rucksack undress

Challenging words for blending
tru<u>n</u>k dru<u>n</u>k sku<u>n</u>k minim<u>u</u>m hundr<u>e</u>d sudd<u>e</u>n tantr<u>u</u>m pupp<u>e</u>t trumpe<u>t</u>

Phrases and sentences for reading
a red sunset   mud on a rug   ducks on a pond   a hot mug

ie ee or z w ng v oo **oo** y x ch sh th **th** qu ou oi ue er ar

I

Words for blending, segmenting and dictation
lap lit let leg log pal lip lot lid lad plot plop gulp lamp land plus split lump lend tilt clap clip lost help held list melt limp plan plug plum glum glad slug slid slim slip slit slot slam slap lent stilt spilt spelt clamp clump clog slept plump adult solid until unless unplug laptop insult limit splendid plastic electronic clarinet halal

Words for blending only
pill kill hill tell mill sell dull gull mill till sill dill bell gill ill lick luck lock silk sulk milk click clock skill skull elk kilt lass smell spell less spill still loss unlock lipstick

Challenging words for blending
li<u>n</u>k pla<u>n</u>k helpl<u>e</u>ss helm<u>e</u>t <u>a</u>llotm<u>e</u>nt plan<u>e</u>t n<u>e</u>glect pelic<u>a</u>n s<u>e</u>lect tripl<u>e</u>t cat<u>a</u>pult lem<u>o</u>n mel<u>o</u>n less<u>o</u>n anim<u>a</u>l tins<u>e</u>l car<u>o</u>l tunn<u>e</u>l hospit<u>a</u>l cor<u>a</u>l c<u>o</u>llect eld<u>e</u>st <u>e</u>lectric <u>e</u>lastic milkm<u>a</u>n

Phrases and sentences for reading
spilt milk   a lost dog   a plastic cup   a splendid sunset
a slim man   Can Sam lend a hand?   A cat laps up milk.

s a t i p n c k e h r m d g o u l f b ai j oa

f

Words for blending, segmenting and dictation
fun fog fat fan fed fig if elf soft lift loft fist felt film fact fond gift
sift self flop flip flan drift font fund tuft himself infect frantic fantastic

Words for blending only
fell fill fuss cuff tiff huff puff stiff fluff gruff sniff cliff off flick frock
traffic puffin muffin

Challenging words for blending
affect frank infant adrift gorilla difficult daffodil confident forest

Phrases and sentences for reading
a fun run   lift off   a soft tuft   a cat flap   a red flag
a fantastic gift   a fat frog on a log   flip flops   huff and puff

b

Words for blending, segmenting and dictation
cub bad bat bib bag rub bit bin pub bed bud bug big bet bun beg
rob but bus belt bump crab scab club bend bent best bulb grab
grub blend blond robin habit

Words for blending only
back brick black block bill bell rabbit boss

Challenging words for blending
brink bank absent abrupt bucket blanket bottom blossom albatross
dustbin subtract umbrella

Phrases and sentences for reading
bed bugs   a bad back   ten black bats   a crab on a rock
a big red bus   a black handbag   a big black rabbit

ie ee or z w ng v oo **oo** y x ch sh th **th** qu ou oi ue er ar

ai

Words for blending, segmenting and dictation

fail laid maid bait paid pain gain raid rail main hail mail nail pail rain sail tail aid ail aim plain trail strain faint paint brain claim drain train grain sprain saint snail stain raindrop

Challenging words for blending

a̲cclaim re̲main co̲mplain co̲ntain o̲btain aiml̲ess a̲gain a̲fraid a̲gainst

Phrases and sentences for reading

a cat's tail   a big brain   a snail trail   Get on a train.
Paint it black.   A big raindrop land̲s on an umbrell̲a.

j

Words for blending, segmenting and dictation

jet jog jam job jug jut jig jot jab just jump object subject project

Words for blending only

jack

Challenging words for blending

ju̲nk jack̲et

Phrases and sentences for reading

a big jump   just a drop   a milk jug   a traffic jam
red jam   a big project   A cat jumps and land̲s on a rock.

s a t i p n c k e h r m d g o u l f b ai j oa

oa

Words for blending, segmenting and dictation

goat boat load soap foam toad road loaf coat moan moat roam toast coast roast groan float boast oat unload raincoat

Words for blending only

oak cloak croak soak

Challenging words for blending

afloat soapsuds crossroads

Phrases and sentences for reading

a big road   jam on toast   a goat in a boat   a rip in a red raincoat
A toad croaks.

ie

Words for blending, segmenting and dictation

pie tie die lie lied tried dried cried spied tied fried untie magpie

Words for blending only

terrified

Challenging words for blending

cries fries tries flies dries

Phrases and sentences for reading

a hot pie   a red tie   ten flies in a tent   A man cries.
A magpie flies.   Ben lies in bed.

14

ie ee or z w ng v oo **oo** y x ch sh th **th** qu ou oi ue er ar

ee

Words for blending, segmenting and dictation

bee see seed need feet deep heel beef jeep peep reef reel feel feed meet seen been beep reef seem reed reel tree free eel greed steel sleep green speed screen steep bleed greet creep street indeed canteen

Words for blending only

keen leek seek peek settee coffee toffee keep creek

Challenging words for blending

asleep agree agreement disagree

Phrases and sentences for reading

deep sleep   a steep hill   a free spirit   an eel in a coral reef

bees in a tree   A tree needs a seed.

or

Words for blending, segmenting and dictation

for sort torn horn corn cord born fort form port lord or sport storm snort inform foghorn landlord platform portrait popcorn record

Words for blending only

cork fork stork corridor

Challenging words for blending

afford report organ forbid forget forgot support sportsman important ornament doctor transport anorak tractor

Phrases and sentences for reading

a fun sport   hit or miss   a fork in a road   a port in a storm

platform ten

s a t i p n c k e h r m d g o u l f b ai j oa

Z

Words for blending, segmenting and dictation
zip zit zap zest zigzag

Words for blending only
buzz fizz jazz buzzcut

Challenging words for blending
zebr<u>a</u>

Phrases and sentences for reading
zip it up   a buzzcut   a red zigzag   a jazz club
Bee<u>s</u> buzz in tree<u>s</u>.   Zac zips up hi<u>s</u> jack<u>e</u>t.

W

Words for blending, segmenting and dictation
win web wet wag wig weed wind went swim swam twig twin worn
wait twist sweep sweet swept waist wail wilt swift west weep wept
tweet wombat wigwam cobweb windscreen sweetcorn waistcoat

Words for blending only
wick well week will swell unwell weekend windmill

Challenging words for blending
wi<u>n</u>k b<u>e</u>tween witn<u>e</u>ss waitr<u>e</u>ss

Phrases and sentences for reading
a big twist   a green weed   a west wind   flie<u>s</u> in a cobweb
Sit b<u>e</u>tween us.   A fat magpie snaps a twig.

ie ee or z w ng v oo oo y x ch sh th th qu ou oi ue er ar

ng

Words for blending, segmenting and dictation
ring sing bang song wing hang gang long sung rang sang rung hung lung sling fling flung clang cling sprang swung sting spring bring swing stung strong string morning freezing seeing sleeping weeping feeling painting ping-pong landing meeting oblong promising railing ding-dong speeding training jumping

Words for blending only
king willing wedding sitting buzzing spelling smuggling swelling soaking running

Challenging words for blending
along belong stinking snoring

Phrases and sentences for reading
a big bang   a freezing morning   a long string   Sing us a song.
Hang on!   Let sleeping dogs lie.

v

Words for blending, segmenting and dictation
van vet vat vest vent vain anvil livid vivid advent invent vomit victim invest

Challenging words for blending
develop venom vitamin devil level velvet caravan vanilla travel visit seven driven

Phrases and sentences for reading
a vivid red   a green vest   a vent in a tent   a black van
a velvet jacket   a van on a long road

s a t i p n c k e h r m d g o u l f b ai j oa

oo

Words for blending, segmenting and dictation
good wood soot foot hood woof wool stood footsteps

Words for blending only
cook hook rook took book crook brook scrapbook

Challenging words for blending
woolle̲n woode̲n woodla̲nd

Phrases and sentences for reading
a long book   footsteps in sand   a big cookbook
a brook in a wood   A cat looks at a rat.

Words for blending, segmenting and dictation
boo zoo moo too poo hoof mood food moon loop root soon boot
hoop roof room zoom toot boom hoot noon spoon broom scoop
bloom gloom proof stoop droop roost swoop bedroom beetroot igloo

Words for blending only
spook cloakroom tattoo broomstick

Challenging words for blending
foo̲l poo̲l coo̲l too̲l stoo̲l toadstoo̲l ra̲ccoon ba̲boon

Phrases and sentences for reading
a cat on a roof   food for goats   a man in a bad mood
a moon rocke̲t   a broom for sweeping   a crab in a rock poo̲l

ie ee or z w ng v oo **oo** y x ch sh th **th** qu ou oi ue er ar

y

Words for blending, segmenting and dictation
yes yap yet yam yum yelp

Words for blending only
yak yell yuck

Challenging words for blending
ya<u>n</u>k

Phrases and sentences for reading
not yet   a sick yak   yum or yuck   a big yelp
A dog i<u>s</u> yapping.   Dev i<u>s</u> yelling for help.

x

Words for blending, segmenting and dictation
six fox fix box wax fax tax ox mix next text exit flex explain extend expand index mailbox paintbox sixteen boxing extinct expect

Words for blending only
express textbook

Challenging words for blending
e<u>x</u>am unexpect<u>e</u>d hex<u>ago</u>n vix<u>e</u>n experim<u>e</u>nt r<u>e</u>lax maxim<u>u</u>m too<u>l</u>box

Phrases and sentences for reading
six ducks on a pond   a man in a boxing ring
A red fox sits in a box.   Mix it up.

s a t i p n c k e h r m d g o u l f b ai j oa

ch

Words for blending, segmenting and dictation

chin chap chip rich chop chat such much punch bench bunch lunch munch pinch chimp chest champ chug chain torch hunch inch poach porch speech trench drench finch chump chimpanzee ostrich coach crunch screech

Words for blending only

chick chill check cheek chopsticks duchess chaffinch chess cockroach

Challenging words for blending

fetch switch chunk attach chicken children sandwich chickenpox chipmunk approach

Phrases and sentences for reading

a rich man   chips in a bag   chopping wood   a long chain
a choo-choo train   an ostrich in a zoo   a hen and six chicks

sh

Words for blending, segmenting and dictation

fish shop dish wish ship hush rush shed shut rash mash dash shot shut shelf brush smash flash flush fresh shoot sheep sheet short shrimp splash finish paintbrush punish shampoo mushroom ash shin shift shrug flesh polish posh publish selfish shred slush vanish blush crush cash crash

Words for blending only

shell shock shook shall eggshell rubbish bookshop shellfish shrill

Challenging words for blending

refresh astonish shrink shrank shrunk

Phrases and sentences for reading

ten fish in a pond   a crash landing   sixteen books on a shelf
I am in a rush.   I wish I had a map.   I am shopping for shampoo.

ie ee or z w ng v oo **oo** y x ch sh th **th** qu ou oi ue er ar

th

Words for blending, segmenting and dictation
this that then with them than smooth within

Phrases and sentences for reading
this and that   a dog with a long tail   Look at this smooth rock.
This cat can swim.   Meet them next week.   I went on a run with them.

Words for blending, segmenting and dictation
thin moth pith tenth thing thud thump tooth teeth three thorn throat
maths faith length north thrush froth broth throb theft strength
toothbrush cloth

Words for blending only
thrill thick

Challenging words for blending
width sixth think thank anthem arithmetic pathetic marathon

Phrases and sentences for reading
six moths   thanks a lot   a thin string   thick socks for boots
a prick from a thorn   a maths book   **the** tenth shop on **the** street
Thank him for **the** presents.   The book fell with a thump.

s a t i p n c k e h r m d g o u l f b ai j oa

qu

Words for blending, segmenting and dictation

quiz quit queen quilt liquid quail squid squint quench quest tranquil

Words for blending only

quill quick quack quicksand

Challenging words for blending

squirr<u>e</u>l <u>e</u>quipm<u>e</u>nt r<u>e</u>quest

Phrases and sentences for reading

a quick quiz   a thick liquid   A duck i<u>s</u> quacking.   a strong queen

i<u>n</u>k from a squid   **He** will win **the** quiz.   **She** kept a pet squid.

He steps in quicksand.   **She** i<u>s</u> on a quest.   **She** quits.

ou

Words for blending, segmenting and dictation

out loud ouch noun found shout mouth round count sound proud
scout cloud pound spout ground sprout without outing hound couch
crouch pouch south stout slouch snout trout wound joust outstanding

Words for blending only

background outfit

Challenging words for blending

<u>a</u>mount <u>a</u>loud <u>a</u>bout <u>a</u>round round<u>a</u>bout <u>a</u>ground <u>a</u>ccount <u>a</u>ccount<u>a</u>nt
ou<u>r</u> sou<u>r</u> flou<u>r</u>

Phrases and sentences for reading

north or south   a loud sound   without fail   big rain clouds

lost and found   green sprouts   **We** found a lost cat.

Help **me** out.   Meet **me** in **the** classroom.   **We** need outfits.

ie ee or z w ng v oo oo y x ch sh th **th** qu ou oi ue er ar

oi

Words for blending, segmenting and dictation
oil boil soil join coin coil joint point spoil spoilt foil moist toil void
oilcan boiling spoilsport tinfoil topsoil

Challenging words for blending
dis<u>a</u>ppoint toil<u>e</u>t <u>a</u>void ointm<u>e</u>nt poi<u>so</u>n

Phrases and sentences for reading
boiling oil   rich soil   an odd coin   Point it out.   **He** can **be** a spoilsport.
Join in with us.   **She** will **be** dis<u>a</u>point<u>e</u>d.   **She** will **be** joining us.

ue

Words for blending, segmenting and dictation
due cue hue argue rescue value continue

Challenging words for blending
fu<u>e</u>l du<u>e</u>l sta<u>t</u>ue barb<u>e</u>cue av<u>e</u>nue

Phrases and sentences for reading
a quick rescue   fu<u>e</u>l for a car   a red hue   a poo<u>l</u> cue
We argue a lot.   She will continue.   That **was** a long av<u>e</u>nue.
It **was** good value.   We rescued the cat in the tree.

*For words where ‹ue› makes an /oo/ sound, turn to page 40.

s a t i p n c k e h r m d g o u l f b ai j oa

er

Words for blending, segmenting and dictation

her term verb herb herd fern perm ever stern sister mister silver winter never order river under herself blister splinter painter thunder bumper hamster jumper monster shiver temper toaster thunderstorm understand number singer boiler bother enter perch tender blender blunder slither amber adverb advert sprinter entertain expert antler archer gander gangster border duster gather hanger hoover internet lantern liver lobster member mermaid modern perhaps pester porter printer proper quiver rooster shelter slender slither sooner tavern timber trainer transfer twister jester understood waiter underground chapter evergreen perform misunderstanding corner clever perfect helicopter consider counter scooter

Words for blending only

litter pepper letter better butter fatter supper hotter summer winner ladder dinner hammer pattern robber rubber runner shudder sticker toddler buttercup chatter slipper stagger shatter flutter cracker dagger glitter gutter matter mutter otter kerb spanner locker interrupt rudder scanner scatter potter bitter smuggler stammer stopper stutter suffer trigger upper copper manner swimmer jerk woodpecker cooker offer

Challenging words for blending

anger hunger finger forever propeller terminal customer angler interest dessert tanker afternoon remember trousers lavender asteroid together alert person desert herdsman prefer asterisk conker referee supporter surrender tweezers

Phrases and sentences for reading

black pepper   a long letter   a big bad monster   a never-ending summer
Mermaids sit on rocks.   He sends a letter **to** me every week.
She got **to** chapter three.   Her **to do** list **was** long.   **Do** not drop litter.

ie ee or z w ng v oo **oo** y x ch sh th **th** qu ou oi ue er ar

ar

Words for blending, segmenting and dictation
arm arc art bar far jar tar arch barn card cart charm chart dart farm
hard harm harp harsh argue march marsh part sharp scar star tart
yard scarf artist barber darling farmer larder partner sharper smart
start garlic armband farmyard starfish starling cartoon

Words for blending only
ark bark dark mark park shark spark darkroom March

Challenging words for blending
alarm apart apartment arson barbecue blizzard cardigan carpenter
carpet carthorse familiar garden harvest harmless kangaroo market
pardon sharpener similar target tartan ajar buzzard lizard

Phrases and sentences for reading
a jar in a larder   goats in a barn   ten sharks with sharp teeth
a pink starfish   A dog barks in a park.   A car parks in a farmyard.
Shark teeth **are** sharp.   Rocks **are** hard.   He took **all** the jam tarts.
I think **all** cats **are** smart.

y a_e e_e i_e o_e u_e ay oy ea y igh ow ow ir

Alternative Letter-Sound Spellings

‹y› as /ee/

‹a_e› as /ai/

‹e_e› as /ee/

‹i_e› as /ie/

‹o_e› as /oa/

‹u_e› as /ue/

‹ay› as /ai/

‹oy› as /oi/

‹ea› as /ee/

‹y› as /ie/

‹igh› as /ie/

‹ow› as /oa/

‹ow› as /ou/

‹ir› as /er/

‹ur› as /er/

‹ew› as /ue/

‹aw› as /or/

‹au› as /or/

‹al› as /or/

‹ph› as /f/

soft ‹c›

soft ‹g›

‹ue› as /oo/

‹u_e› as /oo/

‹ew› as /oo/

‹air› as /air/

‹ear› as /air/

‹are› as /air/

ur ew aw au al ph c g ue u_e ew air ear are

⟨y⟩ as /ee/

Words for blending, segmenting and dictation

body dusty frosty rusty ugly filthy very greedy grumpy handy windy lumpy misty party pity plenty sadly sandy sleepy lily soapy stormy gusty army daily frothy elderly rugby property mainly pantry roomy entry shortly simply copy study sporty teeny creepy hardy speedy

Words for blending only

holly jolly daddy funny poppy bunny silly dolly puppy nanny fussy rocky jelly runny sunny tummy lorry dummy lucky penny teddy berry nappy cherry foggy muddy floppy buddy buggy granny spotty dizzy happy grubby hurry wobbly marry potty merry milky yummy soggy sorry sticky tricky unhappy unlucky carry curry skinny spooky stuffy tabby hobby ferry fuzzy glossy jellyfish silky tubby wiggly willingly woolly

Challenging words for blending

sto<u>r</u>y partly arch<u>e</u>ry art<u>e</u>ry cutl<u>e</u>ry em<u>p</u>ty ha<u>n</u>ky wo<u>n</u>ky acad<u>e</u>my ag<u>o</u>ny dai<u>s</u>y annivers<u>ar</u>y <u>a</u>stron<u>o</u>my ma<u>je</u>sty ma<u>jor</u>ity mem<u>or</u>y en<u>e</u>my fact<u>o</u>ry hist<u>or</u>y vict<u>o</u>ry indu<u>s</u>try terrific<u>a</u>lly territ<u>or</u>y simil<u>ar</u>ly satisfact<u>or</u>y clum<u>s</u>y slipp<u>er</u>y pott<u>er</u>y crock<u>er</u>y lott<u>er</u>y robb<u>er</u>y silv<u>er</u>y noi<u>s</u>y slipp<u>er</u>y <u>a</u>strol<u>o</u>gy sto<u>r</u>ybook poss<u>i</u>bly happ<u>i</u>ly fam<u>i</u>ly terr<u>i</u>bly char<u>i</u>ty activ<u>i</u>ty

Phrases and sentences for reading

a lucky penny   a yummy curry   a very sleepy bunny   an elderly granny
A frog jumps off a lily pad.   We **are** lucky.   She ha<u>s</u> a party dress.
Malik and Lily **are** funny.   She had a wobbly tooth.

y a_e e_e i_e o_e u_e ay oy ea y igh ow ow ir

⟨a_e⟩ as /ai/

Words for blending, segmenting and dictation

ate ape ale game lane gate save gave came cave case cane made name hate safe tale jade wave date pale late same gale sale tame tape rate male mane mate maze gaze pane lame wade fame fade daze grape flame plate plane brave crane scrape spade stale blame graze chase shame shape shave shade frame grade blade blaze slate state trade grave invade inhale inflate sunshade estimate exterminate imitate lampshade indicate landscape caveman scale complicate

Words for blending only

cake rake bake lake make wake take snake skate brake pancake handshake mistake cornflakes fake nickname irritate shake

Challenging words for blending

later paper wafer blazer inhaler sandpaper relate operate escape marmalade lemonade pavement decorate amaze hesitate approximate ashamed demonstrate translate awake

Phrases and sentences for reading

snake scales   a big mistake   a dinner plate   He bakes a cake.
She makes pancakes.   She ate **all** your cornflakes.   Wake up.
Come and pick **some** grapes with me.   She **said** we must be brave.
Let's bake a cake.   **You** can **come** back **here** later.
She **said** her name.   **They** look for **some** bats in a cave.

ur ew aw au al ph c g ue u_e ew air ear are

‹e_e› as /ee/

Words for blending, segmenting and dictation

eve theme evening athlete extreme concrete

Words for blending only

extremely

Challenging words for blending

ev<u>e</u>n unev<u>e</u>n met<u>e</u>r fev<u>e</u>r d<u>e</u>lete the<u>se</u> tr<u>a</u>peze c<u>o</u>mpletely c<u>o</u>mplete c<u>o</u>mpete

Phrases and sentences for reading

a theme park   a sunny evening   an extreme sport   a tr<u>a</u>peze artist

An athlete c<u>o</u>mpetes in the long jump.   It was extremely spooky.

Will **they** join us **here** this evening?   **There are** ev<u>e</u>n better grapes **here**.

y   a_e   e_e   i_e   o_e   u_e   ay   oy   ea   y   igh   ow   ow   ir

‹i_e› as /ie/

Words for blending, segmenting and dictation
ride hide nine ripe life five line pipe mile pile tile file dive time vine side wipe fine bite hive wide size mine wine tide wife live quite shine prize smile drive slide bride inside upside bedtime invite outside stripe beehive sunshine slime bedside divide glide pride reptile thrive spine tribe underline website swipe

Words for blending only
like bike kite lakeside likely dislike spike strike unlike unlikely hillside hike lively

Challenging words for blending
fire wire bonfire spire spider tiger glider hibernate umpire vampire arrive alike alive crocodile wise bridesmaid advertise item arise appetite describe organise pantomime rise polite provide refine revise satellite silent sunrise clockwise unwise beside wives

Phrases and sentences for reading
Spiders hide outside.   **They** ride bikes.   a tiger with nine stripes
It is time for bed.   Snail slime makes a trail.   **They** went inside.
There was **some** time left to finish the game.   We went for a drive.
You run twenty-six miles in a marathon.

ur   ew   aw   au   al   ph   c   g   ue   u_e   ew   air   ear   are

‹o_e› as /oa/

Words for blending, segmenting and dictation
code cone close bone home rope hope note doze lobe robe tone zone wove stone drove slope throne owe explode stove trombone alcove

Words for blending only
poke joke woke stroke smoke broke choke spoke homemade milestone lonely

Challenging words for blending
over sole mole hole pole role stole flagpole tadpole antelope voter hose rose nose close those alone primrose propose stethoscope suppose telescope open enclose broken awoken molehill antidote oversleep overcoat overlook overtake leftovers October

Phrases and sentences for reading
a smoke alarm   a queen on her throne   a frog with five tadpoles
A mole hides in a molehill.   Antelopes roam in herds.   She was lonely.
This tadpole will soon **become** a frog.   He spoke softly.

y a_e e_e i_e o_e u_e ay oy ea y igh ow ow ir

‹u_e› as /ue/

Words for blending, segmenting and dictation

cube cute mute tune tube fume nude use volume perfume costume

Words for blending only

duke attitude

Challenging words for blending

use mule excuse fuse refuse accuse amuse assume unused used
useless confuse fortune computer

Phrases and sentences for reading

a computer game   a costume for a party   a cute bunny   a red cube
a bad attitude   He was in costume.   The computer was broken.
She sang **all** the notes in the tune perfectly.   It was the best perfume.

*For words where ‹u_e› makes an /oo/ sound, turn to page 41.

‹ay› as /ai/

Words for blending, segmenting and dictation

bay ray day hay lay pay may say way play tray stay clay pray sway
slay stray spray staying yesterday runway holiday playground player
display playpen subway stingray crayon crayfish hooray

Words for blending only

midday weekday haystack playtime daytime driveway railway May

Challenging words for blending

away layer sideways

Phrases and sentences for reading

hip hip hooray   playtime in the playground   my red crayon
A stingray was swimming in the bay.   Stay away from the railway tracks.
There **is one** day left until we **go** on holiday.   Yesterday was Sunday.

ur ew aw au al ph c g ue u_e ew air ear are

‹oy› as /oi/

Words for blending, segmenting and dictation
boy soy toy joy enjoy employ employer employee oyster

Words for blending only
joystick

Challenging words for blending
soya annoy annoying ahoy employment joyful destroy royal

Phrases and sentences for reading
an oyster shell   That boy likes cake.   You can win a toy.
Do you enjoy painting?   That toy rabbit is **so** cute.

‹ea› as /ee/

Words for blending, segmenting and dictation
eat tea sea pea meat read each beat heap leaf mean heat seat
team leap lead neat bead bean beam east feat flea lean seam reach
clean cream peach cheap stream least teach steam dream yeast
beach scream peanut treat eager teapot seatbelt meaning teabag
teacher teaspoon underneath steamship anteater seafood teacup

Words for blending only
beak leak weak bleak peak sneak speak creak peacock squeak
seagull seashell seasick daydream seaside meantime seaweed

Challenging words for blending
seal easy easily jeans weasel appeal season reason weakness
treatment weaken leaflet repeat reveal really clear near real heal
meal deal steal

Phrases and sentences for reading
east or west   seaweed on a beach   the **old** teapot with a crack in it
That seal **only** eats fish.   A flea jumps onto a cat.   Anteaters eat ants.

y a_e e_e i_e o_e u_e ay oy ea **y** igh ow ow ir

⟨y⟩ as /ie/

Words for blending, segmenting and dictation

by my cry try fly dry fry shy sty sly spy myself nylon satisfy magnify multiply simplify pylon typing

Words for blending only

sky butterfly terrify terrifying

Challenging words for blending

reply apply python supply dragonfly lullaby skyscraper rely

Phrases and sentences for reading

a red butterfly   a silver skyscraper   a sly **old** fox   a green dragonfly
They fly kites in the cloudless sky.   They **have** a pet python!
We **have** to try.   Try it out for yourself.   She is a spy!

⟨igh⟩ as /ie/

Words for blending, segmenting and dictation

high sigh night light right sight bright fight tight thigh midnight might fright flight slight tights upright sunlight lamplight highlight fortnight lightning nightdress

Words for blending only

slightly tightrope

Challenging words for blending

tighten frighten overnight nightingale

Phrases and sentences for reading

a bright light   the match highlights   thunder and lightning
Meet us at midnight.   Bats **only** fly at night.
She had a fright in the night.   I might spend it all.

ur   ew   aw   au   al   ph   c   g   ue   u_e   ew   air   ear   are

‹ow› as /oa/

Words for blending, segmenting and dictation
low bow mow tow sow row slow snow crow blow flow glow show grow own throw window shadow owner elbow rainbow grown-up lower rowing shown snowman snowstorm thrown widow widower

Words for blending only
yellow borrow pillow follow narrow arrow snowflake shallow marrow hollow sorrow sparrow willow windowsill fellow bellow marshmallow snowy windowpane

Challenging words for blending
below slowest bungalow lowest tomorrow overflow

Phrases and sentences for reading
a rowing boat   a yellow pillow   a snowy day   a bow and arrow
A crow and a sparrow that **live** in the same tree.   Look at that snowman.
A willow tree swaying in a snowstorm.   A crow sleeps in a nest.

‹ow› as /ou/

Words for blending, segmenting and dictation
cow how now bow row brown down town drown crown clown crowd frown shower flower powder power tower sunflower gown flowerpot however cowshed

Challenging words for blending
owl allow towel coward trowel vowel overcrowded scowl prowl growl howl fowl

Phrases and sentences for reading
flower power   a yellow sunflower   a queen with a crown
Trees and flowers like a light shower.   A tiger prowling around a tree.
Give the brown cow some hay.   An owl hunts at night.

y a_e e_e i_e o_e u_e ay oy ea y igh ow ow **ir**

‹ir› as /er/

Words for blending, segmenting and dictation

fir sir bird girl dirt stir firm first shirt third chirp birth twirl swirl songbird squirt thirst thirteen birdseed

Words for blending only

skirt stirring shirk blackbird thirsty birthday dirty thirty firmly

Phrases and sentences for reading

first and third   It **was** her thirty-first birthday.   A girl stirs her tea.
A **little** songbird chirps happi_ly_ in a fir tree.   The girl came first.
A girl fell **down** in the dirt.   Can we go to the birthday party?

‹ur› as /er/

Words for blending, segmenting and dictation

fur turn burn hurt surf turf churn burnt burst church sunburnt turning disturb murmur suburb unhurt turnip yogurt

Words for blending only

purr furry surname survive burger further murder

Challenging words for blending

cur_l_ yog_h_urt burg_l_ar r_e_turn curt_ai_n turb_a_n furth_e_st s_u_rround _a_bs_u_rd hurtf_u_l nurs_e_ry

Phrases and sentences for reading

a burst pipe   Turn it off and on _a_gain.   He hurt himself cooking a burger.
A furry cat cur_ls_ up on my lap and starts purring.   I_s_ the toast burning?
They go surfing.   I_s_ it my turn yet?

| ur | ew | aw | au | al | ph | c | g | ue | u_e | ew | air | ear | are |

‹ew› as /ue/

Words for blending, segmenting and dictation
few new dew stew skew pew newt fewer newer

Words for blending only
skewer curfew

Challenging words for blending
new<u>s</u> v<u>i</u>ew new<u>s</u>pap<u>e</u>r curl<u>e</u>w

Phrases and sentences for reading
a butterbean stew   morning dew   a few pepper<u>s</u> on a skewer
A girl i<u>s</u> reading a new<u>s</u>pap<u>e</u>r.   A newt i<u>s</u> swimming in a pond.
When did you catch that newt?   **What** i<u>s</u> in this stew?
What i<u>s</u> the new plan?   **When** will the curfew start?

*For words where ‹ew› makes an /oo/ sound, turn to page 41.

‹aw› as /or/

Words for blending, segmenting and dictation
law raw saw paw jaw flaw pawn dawn claw thaw lawn draw straw
prawn yawn jigsaw seesaw withdraw spawn drawn outlaw inlaw
sawdust frogspawn

Words for blending only
hawk strawberry sawmill squawk lawnmower jawbone hawthorn

Challenging words for blending
awkw<u>ar</u>d dra<u>w</u>ing awf<u>u</u>l crawl shawl trawl trawl<u>e</u>r draw<u>er</u>

Phrases and sentences for reading
frogspawn in a pond   a red strawberry   a creepy-craw<u>l</u>y under a log
a tig<u>e</u>r claw   A hawk hunts at dawn.   **Where** i<u>s</u> the jigsaw?
Why did you draw that?   We like strawberry milkshake.

y   a_e   e_e   i_e   o_e   u_e   ay   oy   ea   y   igh   ow   ow   ir

⟨au⟩ as /or/

Words for blending, segmenting and dictation
haul fault haunt vault taunt launch

Words for blending only
faulty laundry

Challenging words for blending
automatic author astronaut nautical haunted August autumn

Phrases and sentences for reading
a faulty light bulb   a rocket launch   a haunted cave   a family vault
Dad is hanging out the laundry.   Astronauts are very brave.
Haul in the fish.   **When** will autumn start?

⟨al⟩ as /or/

Words for blending, segmenting and dictation
all hall fall ball wall call tall small mall ballpoint alter

Words for blending only
talk walk chalk stalk

Challenging words for blending
always altogether fallen altar falcon basketball halt scald salt wallpaper
walrus walnut alternate

Phrases and sentences for reading
a ballpoint pen   a small dog on a walk   salt and pepper
a fat walrus with big tusks   A tall girl kicks the ball into the net.
Why are ants so small?   **Where** will the wallpaper go?

ur   ew   aw   au   al   ph   c   g   ue   u_e   ew   air   ear   are

‹ph› as /f/

Words for blending, segmenting and dictation
dolphin phonics

Words for blending only
phone nephew

Challenging words for blending
alph<u>a</u>bet el<u>e</u>ph<u>a</u>nt orph<u>a</u>n tel<u>e</u>phone ph<u>o</u>togr<u>a</u>ph ph<u>o</u>togr<u>a</u>pher ph<u>o</u>togr<u>a</u>phy alph<u>a</u>betical proph<u>e</u>t phant<u>o</u>m phr<u>a</u>se hyph<u>e</u>n

Phrases and sentences for reading
jolly phon<u>i</u>cs   A dolphin swimming in a bay.   A girl talks on her phone.
Which boy i<u>s</u> your nephew?   **Who** i<u>s</u> calling my phone?

soft ‹c›

Words for blending, segmenting and dictation
pincer cancer ulcer

Words for blending only
mice rice nice face race ace lace dice cell place brace trace space twice excite princess officer process sacrifice saucer iceberg spaceship participate anticipate except

Challenging words for blending
excell<u>e</u>nt d<u>e</u>cide s<u>c</u>i<u>ss</u>ors bracel<u>e</u>t <u>a</u>ccid<u>e</u>nt exerci<u>s</u>e cert<u>ai</u>n cell<u>ar</u> surf<u>a</u>ce res<u>i</u>d<u>e</u>ncy r<u>e</u>place r<u>e</u>duce r<u>e</u>cite ancest<u>or</u> <u>a</u>scend intr<u>o</u>duce inn<u>o</u>c<u>e</u>nt decim<u>a</u>l incid<u>e</u>nt cent<u>u</u>ry cer<u>e</u>m<u>o</u>ny c<u>e</u>ment cem<u>e</u>tery cel<u>e</u>brate cancel critici<u>s</u>e c<u>o</u>ncern pharm<u>a</u>cist pencil <u>a</u>dvice vicin<u>i</u>ty sorc<u>e</u>rer graceful su<u>cc</u>ess su<u>cc</u>eed va<u>cc</u>inate a<u>cc</u>ept a<u>cc</u>ent a<u>cc</u>ess circ<u>u</u>s electrici<u>t</u>y cel<u>e</u>ry cent<u>re</u> centip<u>e</u>de d<u>a</u>ncer greengrocer simplici<u>t</u>y

Phrases and sentences for reading
an electrici<u>t</u>y pylon   a cup and saucer   She came first place in the race.
How **many** ice cube<u>s</u> do you like in your dri<u>n</u>k?   I<u>s</u> there **any** rice left?

y   a_e   e_e   i_e   o_e   u_e   ay   oy   ea   y   igh   ow   ow   ir

soft ‹g›

Words for blending, segmenting and dictation
gem germ register margin energetic ginger digit magic origin

Words for blending only
cage wage rage page stage huge energy stagecoach

Challenging words for blending
en̲gage intelligen̲t digita̲l o̲rigina̲l legen̲d gen̲era̲l surgery en̲gaged passen̲ger

Phrases and sentences for reading
a ginger rat in a cage   a huge gem in a crown   Turn to the next page.
They are performing a play on the stage.   Her name was on the register.
She only had one **more** page **before** the next chapter.

‹ue› as /oo/

Words for blending, segmenting and dictation
true clue blue glue sue untrue

Words for blending only
bluebell bluebird

Challenging words for blending
crue̲l i̲ssue ti̲ssue grueso̲me

Phrases and sentences for reading
a blue sky   a crue̲l man   a true sto̲ry   a hot glue gun   He found a clue.
She can fix it with glue.   She **wants** a blue jumper.   **Put** the glue back.
She was sad **because** her bluebird was ill.   He **saw** some bluebell s̲.
He said it was true **because** he **saw** it.

ur ew aw au al ph c **g** ue **u_e** **ew** air ear are

⟨u_e⟩ as /oo/

Words for blending, segmenting and dictation
rude prune flute brute include exclude

Words for blending only
fluke Luke June

Challenging words for blending
r<u>u</u>le sup<u>er</u> rul<u>er</u> s<u>a</u>lute abs<u>o</u>lute p<u>o</u>llute sup<u>er</u>vis<u>e</u> sup<u>er</u>h<u>ero</u>

Phrases and sentences for reading
a rude girl   a long rul<u>er</u>   a sup<u>er</u> day out   abs<u>o</u>lutely **right**
They **were** abs<u>o</u>lutely c<u>o</u>rrect.   The **other** children **should** be includ<u>e</u>d.
We will prune the yew tree in June.   He **could** be rude sometime<u>s</u>.
Would you like to come on holiday with me in June?
Luke broke the only rule.

⟨ew⟩ as /oo/

Words for blending, segmenting and dictation
crew blew grew drew flew threw shrewd slew shrew chew screw unscrew

Words for blending only
corkscrew

Challenging words for blending
jew<u>e</u>l screwdriv<u>er</u>

Phrases and sentences for reading
She threw a ball for her dog.   **Four** weed<u>s</u> grew in my flowerpot.
Two bird<u>s</u> flew by my window.   He grew up slowly.
The girl was unscrewing a screw with a screwdriv<u>er</u>.

y　a_e　e_e　i_e　o_e　u_e　ay　oy　ea　y　igh　ow　ow　ir

⟨air⟩ as /air/

Words for blending, segmenting and dictation
air fair hair pair lair chair flair stair unfair airbag airport airlift hairpin funfair armchair hairbrush haircut airmail

Words for blending only
fairly airline unfairly staircase

Challenging words for blending
airy dairy fairy fairytale hairy repair upstairs downstairs despair disrepair

Phrases and sentences for reading
a fair game   a fairytale with a happy ending   A plane lands at an airport.
He brushes his hair with a hairbrush.   She wins **their** first game unfairly.
This chair is made from fair trade wood.   It looks like a fairytale here.
Once upon a time, there was a good fairy.   Meet us at the airport.
She goes to the funfair every week.

⟨ear⟩ as /air/

Words for blending, segmenting and dictation
wear bear pear tear swear underwear

Phrases and sentences for reading
wear and tear   a grizzly bear   a jar **of** pear jam   **eight** pears on a tree
My dad likes wearing bright tops.   I tear a page out **of** the newspaper.
Some birds catch fish and bears **also** catch fish.   Bears **love** fish.
The cat tears her bed **cover**.

ur ew aw au al ph c g ue u_e ew air ear are

⟨are⟩ as /air/

Words for blending, segmenting and dictation
bare hare care scare dare rare ware glare spare snare share flare
square stare fanfare welfare mare hardware software

Words for blending only
barely farewell scarecrow nightmare

Challenging words for blending
aware beware declare prepare parent carer compare careful

Phrases and sentences for reading
take care   a bad nightmare   be careful
a square cake   **After** such an exciting day, she barely slept.
She said farewell to her parents.

Tricky Words

Blue Tricky Words

I, the, he, she, me, we
be, was, to, do, are, all

Yellow Tricky Words

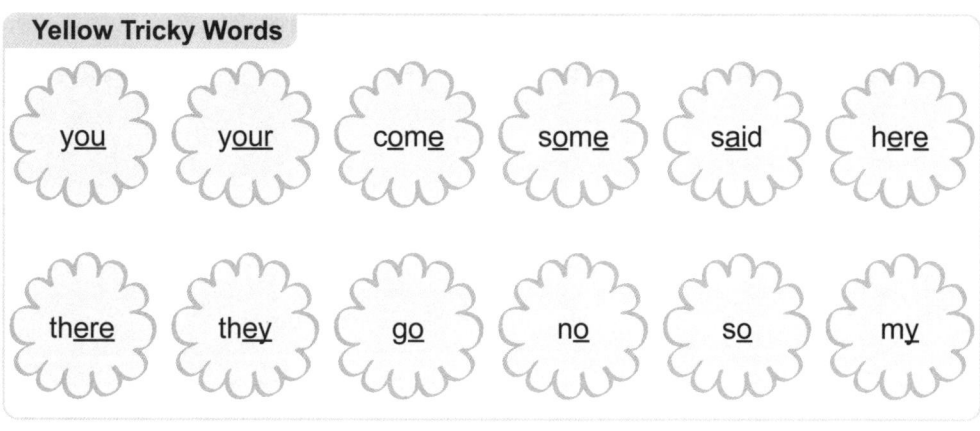

you, your, come, some, said, here
there, they, go, no, so, my

Red Tricky Words

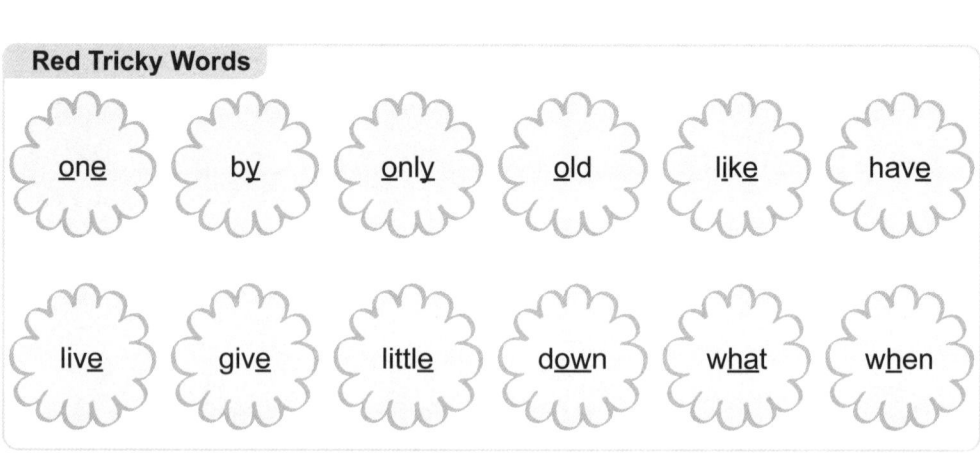

one, by, only, old, like, have
live, give, little, down, what, when

Tricky Words

Green Tricky Words

why • where • who • which • any • many

more • before • other • were • because • want

Pink Tricky Words

saw • put • could • should • would • right

two • four • goes • does • made • their

Brown Tricky Words

once • upon • always • also • of • eight

love • cover • after • every • mother • father

Extra Practice

Developing the skill of blending is an essential skill for learning to read. It requires considerable practice, especially for some children. Similarly with learning to write, extra practice (using dictation) is needed for identifying the sounds in words (segmenting) and writing the letters for those sounds. The Word Bank can be used in a variety of ways to help develop the skills of blending words for reading and writing words from dictation. Children enjoy practising their new skills at home but only when they have the ability to do so. Any homework should be regarded as developing fluency in the skill, and should not be used to introduce or teach the skill.

Alternative Spellings

In particular, children need lots of practice reading and writing words which use alternative spellings. At this stage, the children are not expected to remember how these words are spelt, so only use them in dictation if the children understand which alternative spelling they are practising.

Word Boxes

Select an appropriate range of words from the Word Bank to set out on grids. Print these grids, cut them out and make up word boxes

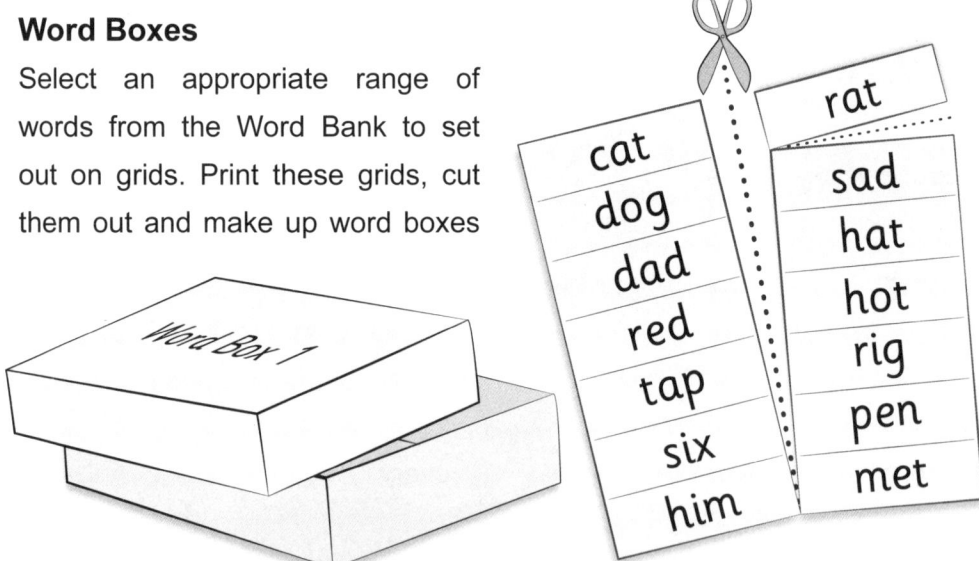

(sets of words can be printed onto coloured card so they can be easily distinguished). When new spellings are introduced, these word boxes can be used for the children to practise  blending. Individual boxes can be made up if a child is having difficulties and needs words tailored to their letter-sound knowledge.

Similarly, phrases and sentences can be set out on grids, printed and cut out to make sets for blending and reading practice. Tricky words can also be introduced at the appropriate stages. Phrases and sentences are more challenging than individual words and practising them helps prepare children for reading books.

Dictation Homework

Parents and carers are keen to help their children with learning to read and write, and are generally supportive of a little homework, whether it is helping their children  read individual words and reading books or writing words, phrases and sentences from dictation. Young children thoroughly enjoy the homework when it is short and it is something they are able to do. The point of the homework is to develop fluency with the skills and not to expect the children to do something that they have been struggling with in class. It works well to make homework voluntary and is best looked on as a bonus rather than a necessity. Similar activities can be used in the classroom, particularly with the children who are struggling and may not get support from home.

Lists of words can be made up and given to children to take home to practise segmenting and writing words from dictation. Working one-to-one with a parent or carer at home can help a child enormously. When sending word lists home, remember to make sure it is clear that the words are for parents and carers to dictate and the children to segment and write by themselves and not to be learnt as whole words. Start with simple consonant-vowel-consonant (cvc) words (e.g. *cat*, *fish*, *sheep*) before moving on to words with initial and final consonant blends (e.g. *crab*, *flag*, *spoon*, *went*, *belt*) and longer regular words. When the children are confident writing words, print out some more sheets with phrases and sentences on. This can be 'voluntary' homework or completed with a helper in school or as a small group activity.

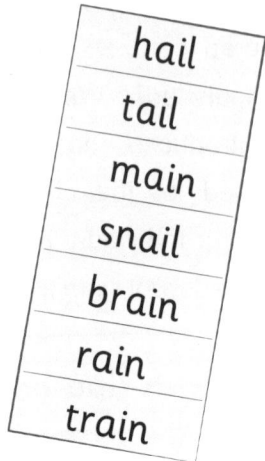

Word Chains

Sit the children in a circle and start off the word chain by saying a word. The child next to you says a word which starts with the sound that the first word ended with, so that a typical word chain might look like this:

Spot the Word

Start by writing a selection of words suitable for blending, segmenting and dictation on the board. Make sure to use a good range of words. Now, read out one of the words from the board and ask the children to identify which word you read out.